Level 1 is ideal for (
some initial reading ir
very simply, using a s
repeated words.

Special features:

flying dinosaurs
teeth
Rex
little dinosaurs
6
7

Opening pages introduce key story words

Careful match between story and pictures

Rex was a big dinosaur.
He saw the little dinosaurs.
They were playing.
"Can I play, too?" said Rex.
"Yes," said the little dinosaurs. "You can play with us."
8
9

Large, clear type

Educational Consultant: Geraldine Taylor
Book Banding Consultant: Kate Ruttle

A catalogue record for this book is available from the British Library

Published by Ladybird Books Ltd
80 Strand, London, WC2R 0RL
A Penguin Company

008
© LADYBIRD BOOKS LTD MMXIII
Ladybird, Read It Yourself and the Ladybird Logo are registered or
unregistered trademarks of Ladybird Books Limited.

All rights reserved. No part of this publication may be reproduced,
stored in a retrieval system, or transmitted in any form or by any means,
electronic, mechanical, photocopying, recording or otherwise,
without the prior consent of the copyright owner.

ISBN: 978-0-71819-464-2

Printed in China

Rex the Big Dinosaur

Written by Ronne Randall
Illustrated by Kim Geyer

flying dinosaurs

little dinosaurs

Rex was a big dinosaur.
He saw the little dinosaurs.
They were playing.

"Can I play, too?" said Rex.

"Yes," said the little
dinosaurs. "You can
play with us."

Rex ran after the little dinosaurs. He snapped his big teeth.

The little dinosaurs were scared. They ran away.

Rex saw the little dinosaurs again. They were playing.

"Can I play, too?" said Rex.

"Yes," said the little dinosaurs. "You can play with us."

Rex roared. It was
a very loud roar!

The little dinosaurs were
scared. They ran away.

Rex saw the little
dinosaurs again.

"Can I play with you?"
he said to them.

"No," said the little dinosaurs. "You are too big. You snap your teeth. Your roar is very loud. We are too scared!"

"Go away," said the little dinosaurs.

Rex went away.
He was not happy.

Then Rex saw some
big flying dinosaurs.
They scared the
little dinosaurs.

Rex ran after them. He roared and he snapped his teeth.

The flying dinosaurs were scared and they went away.

The little dinosaurs were happy.

"Play with us again, Rex!" they said.

Rex did not roar and he did not snap his big teeth.

The little dinosaurs were happy and so was Rex.

How much do you remember about the story of Rex the Big Dinosaur? Answer these questions and find out!

- Who does Rex want to play with?

- Why do the little dinosaurs tell Rex to go away?

- How does Rex scare the flying dinosaurs?